Thin Moon Psalm

Thin Moon Psalm

Sheri Benning

Brick Books

Benning, Sheri, 1977-
    Thin moon psalm / Sheri Benning.

Poems.
ISBN 978-1-894078-60-3

I. Title.

PS8553.E543T44 2007   C811'.6   C2007-902766-0

We acknowledge the Canada Council for the Arts, the Government of
Canada through the Book Publishing Industry Development Program
(BPIDP), the Ontario Arts Council, and the Saskatchewan Arts Board
for their support of our publishing program.

The cover painting is © Grant McConnell, "Between Earth and Sky,"
2006, acrylic on wood, 17.5 inches x 23.25 inches.

The author photograph is by Heather Benning.

The book is set in Sabon and News Gothic.

Design and layout by Alan Siu.

Printed and bound by Sunville Printco Inc.

Brick Books
431 Boler Road, Box 20081
London, Ontario N6K 4G6

www.brickbooks.ca

Larry Joseph Andrew Benning

If I have to leave this place,
I'll go in silence. And if I have to speak,
each word will be small
as a blade of grass, a golden tongue.

– Anne Simpson, "Dunn's Beach"

Contents

Listen

Fall. The season of listening for what we must let go. But your listening was something hungry, a demand to be spoken to. To be heard. Now far from him you remember two things. Probably accidents or undeserved gifts. Like the slant way you realize Spring – weak-tea light of dusk, wrist's moon-shadow when you hold the hot cup. A knowing that slinks through your gaze. But you're doing it again. Please. Just listen.

Driving with him to work. Morning moon passing through pine – sleight of hand, shocks of silver. The story of the farrowing sow. How as a kid he sat in the broth of straw, burnt wood, manure. Furious mewing, steaming birth, he'd place the litter in a box of rags, cut their teeth, return them to their mother. How he and his brothers took turns waiting. Head wrapped in scarves of sleep, he'd break the night-mirror, split light of snow-stars pooled in alloy sky. How he sang stories to stay awake.

You realize you are panicking. You want to free him from the scars of smoke, work, whisky, that tear him from the small songs he made in front of the fire where he learned how to wait.

Listening has made your heart a bruise, a dark pearl of gravity. Outside your cabin, the great blue heron rising each morning, a gesture of abandonment to what is more. It shames you. You watch the moon finally sink into a barbed crown of unlit pine and not rise. That's the only thing you can recall with any sort of clarity – the moon's last time and with such voiceless ease.

What it tastes like

(Frost)

In near dark,
when she's almost
asleep. Smell of coming
rain, wet wool. A spore
of the farm rises in her.
Animals, shadow-pulse.
Her father in the barn.
Rubber boots. Manure.
Open door cedar-light.
Kitchen window weeping
the beet soup loam, sweat
of someone you love. Hands
thick with work and cold
around a hot bowl. Autumn
dusk in bled cloud – loose
straw, spilled oil, a concrete floor.
Steam's in-between-breath pause.
Stars, tin, a drink of well-water.

> *as when you pull a stone from the river,*
> *and hold it in your palm. The light is wrong.*

Filleting

Time redeemed through memory is emotional reality.
    – Larry Benning, study notes on *Four Quartets*, 1967

> *Pike guts, motor oil, milky coffee, birch sap,*
> *passing me flesh on knife-tip, fish scales*
> *stuck to palm – scatter-light,*
> *unfocused eyes,*

Well it was a Heidt from St. Gregor. Big sonofabitch. I was drinking
at the Burr bar by myself and he starts up with me. Oh you know –
"think yer so smart" – shit like that. And I didn't want to fight but
you know how it is, so we head outside. And I get the jump on him.
Mushed his face pretty good. You know slim guys like me gotta do it
hard and do it first. And he starts bawling – bloody embarrassing. So
I pick him up and haul him to the john – through the back so no one
hasta see – and I help him clean up. Then I buy him a beer and tell
him to leave me the fuck alone. Well shit, then the sonofabitch's uncle
starts up with me and he's a big bloody bastard and I'm not there to
fight so I just buy a six-pack to take home. But of course he follows
me out so I just set the beer in the truck box. And he starts dancing
around, thinks he's Cassius Clay, so I ask him if he wants to dance or
fight and he keeps hopping like an ignorant asshole so I kick him a
little – just so he'd drop his hands – and then I plough him one
something furious. And the silly sonofabitch leaned in or something
so damned rights I get him right between the eyes. The poor bugger
walked around with two black eyes for a helluva long time. Anyway
Wilf Chernetsky and them other guys they came to break it up then
but I just left. I guess that Meyer kid who works at the butcher shop
was there. And well shit – next thing he's telling everybody in the
countryside how I beat up both those big sonofabitchin Heidts –

left lid memory-pinched, flex jaw, pose
for the deep-bellied 'huh,' the hang-time vowel
between a story's end and the meaning of it all.
You want him to blink, to shake his head, but

goddamn bunch of bullshit.

he doesn't move.

What Passes Through

November sky: a mouth
that has smoked too much for years. Cold

that could make you bleed, thin
whistle of sun.

Running on scabbed ice. Poplar death,
familiar smell of what passes through dark:

menses   breath   sweat.

That time of day when the membrane
that keeps us separate begins

to fray – sudden rip of the heart,
wolf-flick on the back of the eye.

Errata? Look again. Only the sky's
gaunt skin, but I saw something.

Something that tugs flesh
toward the moon.

Womb

: petal-curled in the garden of my mother,
beneath the moth-drone of her lungs, in her

wish and blood; before my voice became
descent; before language, the sound of distance

between what is divided –

every word I say, traced back to first exile;
every word, rooted in parting; every word

is echo for that moth-drone,
that wish, that blood.

Torn Flesh

"in dead earnest offer the betrayed world a rose"
                                  – Zbigniew Herbert

I want to write how
my lover's eyes imply

                a boy from Haiti

a good harvest, a winter of full-
bellied dream, how his eyes,

                died today,

are a currency that no longer purchases:
penny, kopeck, half-moons

                hatchet deep

of clay under fingernails, horse-hooves,
elm-bark, how

                in his flesh

lying at night in the willow nest of his rib-cage,
next to his corvine heart,

                until he was no more,

I lean into the silty river of his gaze,
see my face reflected –

                a shred of local news –

to say is only to weave
torn flesh, *bright and*

                bloody rags in the dark.

Sleeping Blue

The night before I leave there is a storm. Wind, a train
down Nevsky that runs past us before we can turn
to see what it is. Street dirt bites our eyes,
sunset culled by fists of cloud.

We undress, hold each other urgently; heat of our bodies
a false certainty. Tired and dumb, we whisper small words,
I love you, I love you, pebbles to dam the tide of coming morning.
Forgive us. We don't know how. Love is not inevitable –

when we meet what can't be named, that we choose to love
is a kind of grace that shades everything. Like the soft shadows
of night-snow turning winter into a sleeping-animal blue.

In the morning we take a cab to the airport.
Sky, a bloodless face we can't read, suspect it might be judging us.
We think we might've lacked courage the night before,
though we don't say.

Sometimes I will dream of return, but in the dreams, clouds entropy.
Wind shears your face. And instead of coming home with bread and wine
to find me reading at our kitchen table, a candle gutters
and you will walk away.

At the airport we sit on the steps, share a cigarette.
Without thinking you reach over to wipe something from my lip,
hold your finger there. Later you help me carry my bags through customs,
yell an insult back at the guards before you kiss each of my eyelids,

and promise we'll meet soon. Forgive us, we lack courage.
Don't know how to hold the pose of letting go. But the grace
of the moment on the step, your finger, pressed to my lip,
its small shadow – a sleeping-animal blue.

October Light:

1
Not the flute-song light of April,
of skittish creek waves or
the heart-in-throat jitter
of aspen leaves.

2
When you peel the husk back.

3
Allspice, cinnamon, unwashed hair,
cloves pinned to over-ripe oranges,
sweat of yesterday's labour.

4
Doesn't turn around though it can feel the eyes at its back.

5
Nor is it November's slag-light, the thing said
by a lover that cannot be taken back and now sits
between them broken-winged and awkward.
Not light of the thin-cough after.

6
Inward light –
viscous magma, lamp in a night window,
light of a thought you can't yet say, blood, embers
through the seams of an old wood stove. Light that invites,
go deeper.

7
A thick-tongued drunken prophet, light
that spills long shadows at your feet as if to slur.
It knows how to come to grips with the darkness
that is coming, but it's not going to say.

Lastochka

May 9, 2002

———————

Blood kindles
in the veins of millions; heat
of tense bodies vitrifies the air –

                 glassy sky hovers

above our heads. To watch the Victory Day fireworks
we join the crowd walking down Nevsky Prospekt to Palace Square –
faces blend together, blank as stars.

While he buys us beer from a kiosk, I listen
to some men clustered around guitars.
Mandel'stam believes something as fine as

                 a flute can pull us from our prisons,
can piece together disarticulated days,

but these men strum furiously, their fingers inflamed wicks.
With vein-bulging intensity they shout their songs –

                       all of the cocked triggers
of all the executions during the siege. When he returns,
I reach for his hand,

          his pulse as fine as the curled syllables
his mother calls him, *lastochka* –
small sparrow.

The winter before, *dikaya radost'*:
his shoulder-first walk into night's cold mouth,
Nevsky's light-soaked snow.

Dikaya radost': how I learned to balance words
on teeth and tongue. Diphthongs
subtle as the western meadowlark back home.

Dikaya radost': descent into the labyrinthine strata of the heart,
the heart, that old city. At each turn a talisman – two dawn-grey pigeons
on my sill; their refracted coo, like light through water.

Dikaya radost': untranslatable as children
shucking the day's weight,
their utter, feral joy.

Now, though, difference
in how I hold him –
my arms, an open basket.
                Porous to wind.

Poetry shakes, says Mandel'stam, a lover's hand pulling us
out of sleep. We wake in the middle of a word,
                              a crystal room, where love also means
forcing your child onto a train for Pskov or Novogorood.
Mother-songs, charms in tuliped fists
of children fed to squalls of German soldiers.

We wake where war means a few pieces of bread a day. No heat.
How people survived the Nazi siege
like night-rats –
              only paper-stir, needle-eyes.

We wake where sun is a word rising
                       from the dead; poems, stones
unearthed from the memories of friends. Bound by crystal rooms of words,
poetry forever opens. And *govorit'*, to speak,
means to be always waking.

He stood at our kitchen window when I boiled water for tea. Soon
we'd both return to reading, but for a moment,

in the slow exhale of late afternoon,

he was caught by the absent-minded clouds and the saw-toothed February
wind lifting sodden papers, corners of skirts, in the courtyard. I turned away
from the stove –

on the beaten sill, a rained-on book,
Gogol's *Dead Souls*, which he translated for me –
a lone note of music tries to express bliss
but it in its own echo hears emptiness,

or maybe, he thought, despair.

Stunned by
the barbed cry of a gull,

the imprecision of speech,
how a single word would rip this
light like steam,
my tongue,

a broken wing.

———————

bwili noche:

spare light of a sun
that won't look away while the city undresses –
                   fallen edges, shadow-silk strewn on cobblestone.
Rain-freed smell of lilacs, willow-sap; blade of moon,
grass caught on river-skin, a shiver

in half-lit sky. When he came into the kitchen
to tell me about Shostakovich's alchemy of art –
                         to transcend,
one must bear witness – I thought about Rilke,
after Rodin's counsel: *travailler, rien que travailler,*
                         standing on a quay
in the Neva's alkaline breath, Rilke practiced
how to not look away –

Russia, he thought, ever-changing, never defined,
                         a growing God; to bear
witness, we must transcend ourselves.

Outside the sun still
stooped on candle stubs,
                 the broken city
           horizon. Its thorns of light tore my eyes –
      bone-light of sky
slow cry of the contrite,
rain.

polnoch':
> half-night. Whetstone
for my own word. Midnight
might not be distance measured,
a pilgrim in the middle of a journey,
but a nearing lack or whole. Sky,
a tense blue

> song of balance, a voice that could, at any moment,
fall. I wanted to tell him about watching the city pull away
from a boat on the Neva, faceless buildings, burnt-out embers,
surprised by the city's existence outside of my own.
Like the first time I discovered my mother

> in old letters from a lover. I was ashamed
then as when I watched the old soldiers dancing with the folksingers
under the arch of Palace Square. The waver of their shadow-lank
limbs, the tense beauty of watching what could, at any moment,
fall. The crowd I was voyeur to sang words I recognized
with my head rather than my life.

> The scene reminded me of *Sacrifice*,
the Ciurlionis painting: lamb-smoke when suffering is oblation,
visible only when the city pulled away, but the confused shadows
of bodies cleaved like the folk song's minor key still vibrating in the arch,

> bray without release. I wanted to tell him
about this, but couldn't. The word 'sacrifice' a lie if I spoke aloud.
Something I hadn't considered before.

polnoch':
> nearing lack; nearing whole.

In the looseness of March we walked back
from The Idiot, the basement restaurant named
after that novel. Along the Neva I thought:
                    crocus petals, willow catkins, brome; mouth

sticky with memory, the wet clothes that drown,
my sadness lit
by distance, by belief

in the whole vowel, home. We scried
the mess on the Neva –
                    soaked city light, river-weed, wraiths

of almost remembered dreams. We said our stories
the way they never were,
                    how we wished they could be.
Conscience a wet cold that invades bones.

Remember that painting by Ghe?
                    seed-scatter of early stars and Judas in the shadow of a crowd.
Moon, a bloodless hand, rises up his back,
                                        lights his weight.

Sheathed in salt-sky the engorged sun is the shape of your shock –
awed eye.

How to say the sun over the Neva before
tallow-lit dusk?

Only upon failing to name, can we open up to loss.
The sun is a moment in time

that transcends time. The landmark that dissolves in our blood, tallow-lit dusk,
and somewhere remains whole –

like that cross in the ditch, toothed by wind,
that was always half-way home.

Palace Square. Victory Day. Sky, a grave
that contains us all. I reach for his hand
                    to curl up in the small shadow of his pulse,
but the air shatters,
a fight rips past me – students and skinheads.

A kid wearing orange Doc Martens falls and
one of the skinheads kicks him,
                              breaks his skull.

Someone cries *you bastard*
                        and air tears open:
the skinheads scatter, the dying kid's friends scream
                                for the militia, for an ambulance.

I land on the pavement, head between my knees;
                legs convulse, the orange boots jerk.
I can't look.

Mandel'stam asks us
                does the skull unfold –
temple to temple – so that armies, their soldiers, can flow
through our eyes?

Mikiskaw

The fire which torments us becomes the rose;
our suffering shall be something beautiful.

        – Larry Benning, study notes on *Four Quartets*, 1967

Fall. Running through cougar-shadow light and the clove smell of
summer's death-simmer. Blade of winter held at my throat so I can't see
it, only feel its thin sting on the mothskin of my neck. Soon poplars will
be pleading hands with nothing to hold,

fear-chocked throats. Remember my father in the hospital last year.
Muscle of his work decayed until I found my own body – breastbone
wicker-ridge, colt-knee bulge. Holding his driftwood bones, hands,
a hollow grey, the colour left

when wind peels back light, I had never hated someone more. His limbs
naked but for the whispery hospital cotton, that last bloodless leaf's cling-
by-the-nails desperation. Running now in viscous harvest-sun,

I remember that Cree trappers have a word for this season to come, for
the heldbreathness between gilded leaves and mother-curves of snow, the
waiting for ice to swell at lake's temples.

Moon-hymns

Oh morning moon,
your exiled limp –

spine-bent, eye-on-earth, shedding
yourself along the way. As if

your thinning gaze could ever end
in return. As if the basin of ache

you leave, fossa beneath the braid
of breastbone, could ever be assuaged.

slipped

from earth's pocket,
the stone you pulled

from the shore, forgot
you had, but miss when

you crave something
exact. When the space between

your curled finger and thumb
is a small sadness you want

to fill rather than
look through –

Before we knew your weightlessness,
we did not know how hard

we fall. Unaware of gravity,
time is meaningless; time, the measure

of gravity's gait. Loss of you
is the beginning of speech. Before

there was no need to forage
words, no forest-shadow

of gasped pine,
cried-out leaves.

Oh morning moon,
grandmother's arm

waned by holding water.
Your slow descent

into silence
we call new

shows us our own
slow descent into loss

is birth.

Bird-bones

Air screamed through your bird-bones as you flew
from your snowmobile, into a field of snow and stubble,

once an inland sea. Your spine unhinged.
I stand around the corner of your hospital room,

Andrew, listen to my father sing as he holds your quivering legs.
What emerges from our bodies cracked open? The stiff door

of an abandoned farmhouse: orbit of dust,
flurry of dark wings. Propelled

by the thrum of your heart you landed
in a prairie of frozen stars, my father's song –

the one he sang to me when I fell here, heart-first
and screaming, into the sudden rush of sky.

Descent from the Cross [1]
Rembrandt, 1634
Hermitage Museum
St. Petersburg, Russia

1

The face in the Rembrandt of the man pulling Christ off the cross. It's my
father pacing from the machine shed to the barn. Night diffuse with the
silence of *I have nothing*. Empty-arm begging of autumn fields beneath
sky. Dry snow – flaked stars, moths of reflected light. Wheat two bucks a
bushel. Harvest dust-thin. His body a reed flexed with work and frost. In
the middle of his life, a grief that stops blood.

In the painting, a woman holds a candle. The worn-cotton glow of the
yardlight poorly cloaking the back of night. The man pulling Christ off
the cross is thinking nothing. Not *what should I do? what should I do?*
because to look it in the eye is to die. He's just standing, now in the barn,
the heat of sleeping breath, straw, manure. His bloodless face drifts in the
cadence of animal-pulse. Across his shoulders a burlap sack of feed.
Against his cheek, silence where a heart once beat.

Thin Moon Psalm

Monastery of Christ in the Desert, New Mexico
. . .life consists of love, languor, sweetness, heat and melody. . .
                              – a 13th C. Carthusian Mystic

Wet-feather
moon, half-

sunk in
sun-

frayed
rice grass

           world without –

bone-curved
morning incense

Kyrie

rises in the valley – chamisa,
false mallow, pinyon pine.

eleison
dizzy moon, thin with sorrow-
light, falls beneath dawn

Christe

the shape of hunger –

Sun-sucked cholla-cactus
hull, a many-moth gray.

Where once it drew blood, flute-slits,
hollow smell of heat and weeds.

Later, this is what your voice,
your eyes, what you use in hunger

to enter others,
will be.

slow-blood hills –

You go to bed thirsty. Blood hunched
and staggering up mountain-path veins.
You dream of licking grandfather cliffs,
tongue undoing water that locks stone –

umber faces sliding,
river-ripped valley full,

you dream the end of longing.

In the morning, you walk
fragile on eye-white milk quartz,
earth's ribs raised on convection
currents, in slow-blood hills.

gutted –

The valley unfolds along the river-spine.
You stutter through a maze of desert-

parsley, ice smell of juniper,
wolf-eye-green sage.

Skulls and clay, held in flex
by the weight of time, wear wind-veins.

Thirst throbs on the dark drum, a fire-flower
in the mouth cave, syncopated to the snake heat-hum –

what is wet inside you wants to escape,
to be oblation for the sun.

What is wet inside wants to shuck you –
the gutted sandbar willow, a shed pod,

ecstatic branches of praise.

what scares you –

Moth clenched
on the morning door.
Last night, drone of moon-

leaf wings in exhaled air.
Desire convulsive,

but precise. Now the moth
grips with the silence that holds
stone together.

that song that goes –

Listen
to the Chama river
carry mountains
on its back:

      this is the wood
          of the cross –

      come,
           worship.

going –

You come to a desert to know,
but leave with only rinds of clay,
throat full of psalms, rain-hush

of monks sweeping, straw on stone.
The Chama river, heaving coyote whine,
cragged-light, finds ocean, does not stay.

Somewhere a man heaves us
on his shoulders. Eyes sliced
by a million mirrors, sun

on sand. He still falls
to knuckled rock because we cannot
know; there's only going,
straw on stone.

Fidelity

"At last the fidelity of things opens our eyes"
                    – Zbigniew Herbert

Once my sister was sick. So much had happened to her body
over which she had no say; it lay dormant in her sinew for years.

But then, the aftershock –

I sat beside her when they slipped her body into the MRI.
I wanted to hold her, but couldn't, so I prayed

as though I was a bargain-hunting pauper willing to trade up
glass beads and feathers, something as useless as my life,

for her safety. As though a prayer could be anything
other than a plover's nest in marram grass, vulnerable

to what is always devastatingly unknown.
That night, driving in Saskatoon, she didn't believe

the moon could look like it did, so I drove her to the edge of the city's halo.
Hemmed in by wheat and barley, glow of a bare bulb in the root cellar

of August dusk, we hung our heads out the car windows
into cricket hum. Stars and there it was –

moon, a cupped palm, sallow,
and ready to receive.

Dance

Having tread the same womb,
I know how she moves –

the skin at her nape,
down so fine it can't hold

light, hummingbird
stammer of her bottom lip

when she lies. But watching her
dance, limbs, waves sliding

up a rock face only to descend
and slide again, I realize I know her

as well as a map that says where to go,
but never speaks of the wind-creased linen sky.

After decades in orbit together,
she surprises me with her jackpine-grip

when I threaten to fall, my body,
kindling that holds shape

until it spills under the weight of ash.
In the wash of her body, I think I might never

not-know another this well.

What it tastes like
(Salt)

In the smeared light
of a hardware store,
urine smell of burning
coffee. Against some hip,
the dead-leaf crush of a diaper.
It rises in her. Shadows
threshed by noon sun
implying nothing. A fly
in a bowl of bloated cereal,
sweet milk. Jack-in-the-box
cartoon-caw of a TV left on
a room away. Her father
in a harrow-cloud of brittle
earth. Lilacs, like swollen
lips, in a jam jar. Yesterday's
boiled potatoes. Carrots
in the sink. The metal
taste of dirt. Her mother
in the kitchen, crying.

Her body won't forget. Ridge of skin
after the sloughing of a scab.

Dance

My brother wakes me to tell me about his night: breath,
whisky, smoke, starred December sky. How he danced

with a woman the way I once showed him –
he too misses a body scarred by the same steep

path of birth. We now live a country apart.
Dancing together is rare. Slow hum of heat

echoes the shape of him, lifts me
from a dream of drowning in that creek

west of our farm, where our thirst for return
began, the fetal glow of my face in reeds –

I refuse to let go of the home
we were cast from so I can begin

to breathe. His clove breath,
starred sky, echo of heat,

tell me of night. We now live
a country apart; dancing is rare.

He wakes me to forgive me
for believing my despair

is like no other despair.

Sing

Glass rain of pigeon song
underneath a bridge over the Saint John river –
I don't know how to be here.

Remember last summer?
The autistic boy singing *oh oh oh*. Running
circles around his tent, he became what he thought.

Far away now, you believe if your gaze could lie
in the father-arms of fallow fields, the dull hunger of November
sky, it could rest. Home defined by circles of thought.

In the shards of another's song, remember
the autistic boy's *oh oh oh*. Your own
empty-pocket refrain.

The colour of

The shameless meandering of leaves, the colour of
some slow jazz trumpet, of yeah-i-loved-you-so-
what-ness. A half-step-off, semitone descent.

Somewhere someone is desperately in love with you.
He's trying to slough the shiver of loss with manual labour.
He's painting houses and with every brush stroke he is stabbed
by a memory of *the thinnest blue song*.

How he told you your eyes are the colour of the distance
within an embrace *the thinnest blue song*, in the spring
of a city where the sun doesn't set; between the sky
and the Neva at midnight, *the thinnest blue song*,
that time you took a boat along the Fontonka canal.

His words and the fumes are rotting his brain
as he paints someone's damned house all day, watches
CNN all night, wonders whose bed you're sleeping in, hums
the thinnest blue song the thinnest blue song

and you in this shameless meandering of leaves, the colour of
some cliché for pride, of hold-your-head-high as you fall
at a half-step-off chromatic pace.

November Light:

1

November light, without a home –
back-bent, on the corner of Whyte and 105ᵗʰ
in a torn jean-jacket, cigarette-smoke grey, muttering
at passersby about the darkness that is coming.
Few listen. Few even turn their heads.

2 ʻ

Light of that aborted pig fetus in the dusty quart jar
at the back of the grade ten Biology cupboard.

3

Afraid to open your mail? Shadows
under your eyes? When you think,
do you just get sad?

4

Not October light, the whisky-jack drunk
on fermented crabapples dancing in the dying
flames of the apple tree.

5

Of bone-ash and clay,
which harden into something that can shatter.
If you must, speak in hushed tones.

6

The doe's coat turns dun so she can hide
in the spaces cut by bare aspen branches near
the Saskatchewan river. Only her wet-eyed stare
is visible. November light, something unseen
watching.

Bones in the wings

When he kissed me between my shoulder blades,
I thought how the bones in the wings of birds,
are as fragile as the skim of first frost
on pasture grass – early morning,
late August.

Rift

: pulled to the edge
of the ocean, wan ice
on beach, salt-skiff of tears.

Pine resin, a velvet cloak
of memory. Folds of basalt – once lava
from the mid-Atlantic rift, the shed skin of parting.

Waves open stone, pores that light, with its ethos
of angles, can't know. Places only felt by what is
without borders – water, a lover's breath.

Green curl of new willow, your gaze
at his nape.

In the seed-light of first stars, watch waves forever
enter clefts that were dark secrets and then
watch waves recede.

All fall
his eyes in dusk-lit birch.

Grief in not knowing how much
we still move in those who leave us. Not knowing
how much we're the shape of those we've left behind.

Womb

: there is always a room that we will never return to.
A room shared with a lover in another country.
I come to you at night with few belongings, through moon-
blank faces. In the pace of Nevsky Prospekt,
the infinity of orbit.
Turn the corner.

On the steps of the cathedral that held Dostoevsky, a man
without shoes, charred-dove feet bound in potato sacks.
Turn the corner. Shared breath of train station; snow
exhaling earth, oil, what we leave behind
in our steps, longing for home.

A kitchen – the inside smell of yeast, a tent of sleep, our bodies
when they are animal; sweat gathered where we bend.
Rye bread, wine, tea. Light a candle. Your head in my lap.
In the river-curl of your hair, slow-tongues of city-light and smoke.
Turn the corner for home.

Northern River
c. 1914-1915[2]
Tom Thomson
oil on canvas
155 x 102 cm
National Gallery of Canada

2

Night moved across you like a glacier and you woke here, bone-broken, far from where you thought you would be. If you could tie a string to your what-ifs, this is what they would weave – a hydra-nest of jackpine. The way out of drowning in the foreground is a matter of perspective. You will never read all there is in pine shadow, the dim library of your past. Look through.

Lay aside thinking. Crouch in old blood-stiff sun, moon-ash moss, the thick pelt grief grows. Crouch in the residue of snow, last season's estrus, bark, leaves; melting, a shoot of light in a winter cellar. Wear your past, a pine-shadow mane, across your back. Let your stare be a reaching hand starred with grain. Let the river come to you.

The sudden sound of your name is linked to no one's, heavy as a bird without wings. Tie a string to your what-ifs. This is what they weave – the helix of your pace, a search for certainty, for a dead thing. Choose to love the living. The river is a sweating bone new from the unlit hut of the body; the river is generous, fresh-meated with reflection, balm for forest-bruised feet. Let stiff-back jackpine strip the dross of your stare, your stare a whetted reed. Song will lift from your looking.

Tantramar

: at night you'd lie down beside me;
my body's drift to yours like water, a drawn reflex.
In the morning I'd bring you tea; you'd tell me fine waves of words I murmured,
thin shine of my unfocused eyes. Crescent of iris through pleats of night,
moon in the tantramar of dream.

I thought that I was through with you.
But tonight, sitting by a man, slow static of his hand
in his beard, sound that ends in smoke, my body's drift to you
something I can't control. Your memory on me, thin shine, unfocused eye,
moon in the tantramar of dream.

Notes toward a love poem:

(1)

The night you held my face in your hands, your eyes were the worn metal colour of clouds heavy with snow. In your eyes I could see the season turning.

(2)

Everyone has advice. Sarah says: "Dance wildly, but try to keep one foot firmly balanced on the earth." Though I don't say, I'm afraid this will only make me trip. And I wonder – what would this look like if we weren't so cautious?

(3)

Because my favourite poet, the recluse I told you about, had a lover who, before she was certain they would be together, bought a bed that she knew would fit the length of his body.

(4)

Maybe what's needed is a recipe. Or potion. The kind my sister and I used to stew in old mason jars: yarrow, dandelions, spear grass, water from the rain barrel, July sun. We were just kids, though; magic was possible.

(5)

Later your eyes were the green of morning frost on pasture grass. They reminded me of his in which I first learned to steady my gaze.

(6)

What can I give you? When first snow falls in the pre-dawn hush, softly as moth wings closing, softly as the departure of last night's dreams, the crooked stitches of my grandmother's hand, the quilt-heat of breath, unruly hair, my flushed cheeks, hands here and here, the tender flesh and warmth of my inner thigh. The one high note in "How Great Thou Art," which contains both how to come undone and the path back.

(7)

Because my favourite poet's lover knew for certain all along.

(8)

I should've shown you my heart earlier, but I was embarrassed by how it was dressed in the torn and washed-out cotton of the poor – detritus of last season's poplar leaves and bark. So instead I got drunk. Spoke out of turn. Insulted your friend. Ignored you. I know. I'm not so good at this.

(9)

Because I can't help but wonder what colour your eyes are right now as I listen to the passing cars and the low hiss of night rain on the city streets.

(10)

I haven't written a love poem for years. I don't know if that's what this is. But I want you to tell me your sorrow. And for you to listen to mine. I wish I could sing you all the songs I know – loudly, off-key, and without shame.

(11)

What can I give you? Fiery death of leaves. Deer on a sand bar, the sickle shadows of their bodies on the slowing river. A hot bowl of soup for you to thaw your cold and work-chapped hands against. Root cellar musk of onion, carrots, pepper.

(12)

The more I want to show you, the further away you become. Just try to touch the horizon.

(13)

Because the story you told me about your grandfather. How before the Russians captured him in Greece, he buried beneath a tree his wedding ring and locket, the small, sepia photo of his wife's face.

(14)

Everyone has advice. I know, I know; what I want to believe and the way things are seldom match up. I guess I didn't realize when my fortune cookie read "your romantic obsessions will come true" that this could mean so many different things.

(15)

What's needed is a recipe. Or potion. Outside the glow of the dance hall – breath, cologned-sweat, beer, your hand on my leg while you sing Elvis songs in my ear, the prairie's last gasp of nettle and sage, "love me tender, love me true," and if they could sing along, the stars would sound like crickets.

(16)

"Look," I say. "All's I know is that falling in love, or whatever this is, well, it's always a logistical nightmare." But even as I speak, I know I'll go home to the empty cupboards of uncertainty and old mail. I'll drive too fast to beat the low sky, and though autumn has been exhaling all along, the sudden shift of light to winter will wind me.

(17)

The next day we have an awkward conversation on the patio of some bar. All elbows, and sawdust tongues. I tear apart fallen elm leaves at their seams. You pull a parched flake of leaf from my hair. You love me.

(18)

A recipe. A potion. Something. The rain outside Muenster bar clinging like wet wool. The Weisner boy's worthless and sodden crops. Look south and then east. Beyond that stand of evergreens. See the porch light tunnelling through damp night? That's where my father farmed his whole life. That's where I learned that sometimes there's no choice but to leave.

(19)

You love me not.

(20)

Because on the car ride that day when you pointed to the magpies
teasing currents of air with tail feathers the blue beginning of flame, the
erratic lift and fall of their glide reminded me of my heart at
recognizing the length of your forearm, your one silver hair.

(21)

What can I give you? Funeral pyre of burning stubble, damp grass,
leaves, but then sweet smoke and ash, the rich, black earth of my heart.
All I ask in return: if you notice in the dashboard light that my hair has
fallen in my eyes, that you might hold it briefly between your fingers,
smooth it behind my ear and then linger there.

unsent letter #28

Sarah, tonight a horse-hair moon. A frayed bow cricket-rubbing against the dark string of night. A song of balance that you can only hear if you forget that you can't.

Remember what I had said to you? That trust, like stepping off a mountain –

But Sarah your name reminds me that many years ago, or once upon a time, or maybe I should introduce this differently. Maybe these stories are the dark strings that the eye catches in old movies – the ones we're not supposed to see. The ones that pull.

Though you were in your late nineties, you believed. Inside, your bones shone with new fire, poplars glutted on dawn sun. And another thing –

a stone-curlew, crow-sized, but dustier, always shamelessly singing its name, got sucked into trade winds and was forced to ride across the Atlantic on an empty stomach,

made it to southeastern Spain, the Iberian woodlands: lavender, thyme, oleander, lotus. They found him beneath a lone juniper, wind-burnt, smoking Spanish sage and whistling. Sarah, I ask you such impossible questions –

the great thing about trust, you said, is that its mystery is so much more interesting than knowing. Who can say if God will give you a child? Or that the stone-curlew, high and singing, will take the next train back?

But the bow will drop and when I hear it, the dark note of night will give me that heart-in-the-throat hover of stepping-off. So stop thinking. Hold my hand. Remember, our bones are sated light.

Nocturne

i

His voice –
whisky leaves of dusk
birch, cigarette smoke,
an e minor guitar chord.
Caressing the night-
lake, breath and
call of a loon.

ii

When they tell me about my eyes,   *(green of*
                                    frost on lake's slowing,

I say they are my father's
                    pine smoke and

and when I am old,
                    wolves under November's

they will turn blue.
                    thistle-tine moon).

iii

How we fall –
watching him
split wood,

axe over shoulder,
down the grain of
what joins us.

Wolverine Creek

Fall. When scraped fields
show us the empty-
cathedral air inside us.

Shrew sounds of leaves,
bleeding at a pace the eye can't hold.
As a child standing in willow kindle,

grasses the yellow of grandma's dying
arms, watching geese harrow a sky made
more blue by the radiance of decay,

asking for a sign –
*if you are there, spell this
in the furrow of geese*

and always unable to decode
their flight, to find the equation, a basket
to heap meaning, grandma's apron full of chokecherries,

small questions, *why in death the smell of estrus?*
But soon the geese over Wolverine,
the creek that doglegs our land.

Standing in their wake,
mind made small by another's height,
left with the imprecision of loss –

strewn chokecherries, their bee-sting
taste. Learning we reckon only through
loss: the place where we begin.

Hysterectomy

My mother's head in my lap.
She's crying. Her shirt twists up
beneath her breasts. I trace her
stretch marks, last sun

through bare birch, drifts of fallen
poppy petals at the garden's edge.
Geese knife the dusk sky,
their cries, rusted
hinges. Listen –

winter is a door slowly closing. In the garden,
the poppy's seed pod: cured skull,
my mother's uterus, full
of dried bees.
I trace her

stretch marks, last sun, bare
birch, white of an empty bowl.
Drink her absence,
undivided
light.

Bread, Water

From the well to the porch, the nervous rasp
of boots when snow is clenched tight as glass.

Water to do the day's washing and baking. Look in.
If you can see yourself inside the pocked metal pail,

you understand – water shows you
who and where you are:

faint stars; moon, a pearl
of salt down your brow.

Words, like water, are shaped by gravity if
you can think of gravity as another way of saying

memory. Just as river wearing an elbow-worn coat
of last season's shells and leaves, makes its way

to the ocean, bread is this woman,
before dawn, making enough

for the week. Is the ripple of her
muscles kneading the belly of dough.

Sigh of yeast as she folds each loaf.
Poplar-snap in the wood stove. Steam melting

fronds of window-frost. Aerial-
pitch of stars, pearl-of-sweat-

moon. The word bread,
an estuary. Where tide gathers

river, an old friend, into its arms, pulls it
into heave and the familiar smell of salt.

Bread. Welcome.

St. Benedict's Rule

You make tea for a man who was your lover.
Where once there was desire, now a palm-sized heartbeat,
pleasant to hold. Open wings of frost on the window.

He waits at a table the colour of old teeth.
Outside the abbey's kitchen (a killdeer's nest
in fescue) a blizzard has cried itself to sleep.

Snowdrifts, wide-eyed, torn, at the corners of doors.
Whisper-light of lamp, soft-furred shadow,
metronome-breath of sleep.

You feel the thread of his gaze weave
a tapestry of the ablution that you are
performing for him:

gnawed-on kettle's lost key rattle; damp
cheek of steam; small sounds of pouring water, words
that you murmur when you think no one is looking.

Bark and flower steeping in veined
Wheat Pool mugs. All scraps of shed clothes
from a grandmother's rag-bag, the smell of farm-

chapped hands, diesel, cured clover,
still in her worn poplin, in his worn flannel.
Once he was your lover,

he lived in a cabin on the border
of the abbey's halo. After vespers you'd go
to him. Stars, eyes of birch craning into night.

Wind in evergreens,
a lucid dream, Wolverine Creek
untethered from gravity by sleep.

He lit stubs of old altar candles, showed you how
to play the guitar. Spice of his hair as he knelt before
you: beeswax, wool, smoke. Moon, a blade

sharpened so many times its light grown
soft. The care he took: willow-
balm for feet and hair,

each button
undone, each finger
warmed beneath his tongue.

Legato

-

On the hike down
Tunnel Mountain, creeping-
juniper, wet-eyed berries.

-

Under willow shrub
or larch, the white-crowned sparrow.
What I look for and what in brief moments
approaches, never match up.

-

And though they've been there all along,
bow down to the bowing crocus, lobed petals,
Spring-snow blue, blue of thaw.
Lucent.

-

It was after dinner. Full of the usual sadness, the world
is dying, I just wanted to go to bed. Last breath of dusk,
sun behind the erratic mountain-horizon –
held by a nameless night.

-

White-crowned sparrow legato: breath
through his bottom teeth and beard.

-

He was in shadow singing
the blues. Surprising lift of his voice,
flight from larch, levity of my heart in my throat.

-

Step out.
A black-billed magpie stabs
at bread left on a balcony.

Tail feathers: struck-match-
blue and then green
and then blue.

-

Outside of the ridiculous divisions
of time, Mount Rundle, open-eyed,
mute.

-

When my looking crumbles, rip-rap, the world appears
in fissures. White-crowned sparrow nest, a sipping-cup:
mud, lichens, shred bark, red fescue, leaves.

-

I think I've known him for at least a hundred years.
His song, honey-toned unction. I think I've known him
for at least two thousand years.

-

Song contains us in a light so particular it can't be named –
crocus, struck-match-blue of magpie and then
green and then blue, juniper.

-

In-between-heartbeat brief; when I step out
of my narrow lament; when
the world looks back –

The Breath of Looking

i)

The great horned owl underfeather you found
suspended on brome teaches you about the near
imperceptibility of grief. About thinness.
How light, hardly snared by down,
filters through and changes just-so
and so grief wears you, makes
you its slight shadow.

ii)

The great horned owl underfeather teaches you
about the eyes of someone you long for. How if they could
stroke you, they would be as graceful as the almost
weightless. How if you could look at the sky
through them, you would feel smaller,
but not less.

iii)

The great horned owl teaches you that the knack for
flight has something to do with silence. Its wings polish
planes of air; distance shimmers in their wake. In the after-
weep hiccoughing hearts of poplar leaves, how
to feel the silk breath
of looking.

Amber

: I go to bed early. Weak-muscled.
Stars, faint scars of light behind
closed eyes. I thought memory was

an aphid hover over garden that descends
or does not. I was wrong. Lavender and heat
ease my uterine pulse. Memory held

here, in the resin of my body.
A glass of water, a prayer, a lamp left on,
and behind closed eyes, scars of light,

St. Petersburg from the height of *Kazanski Sabore*.
In sun-thick snow, linen strung between windows
of jaundiced apartments, frozen sheets, empty shells

of wind. Alleys, as palm-veins, paths
to hidden doors. You gave me an amber
stone, memory of Spring. My face held

in sap against your chest in *Letney Sad*,
where we read to Spring-water shine
of new leaves. Memory pulses

until meaning is found.
I wake in forgotten light
to loosened blood.

unsent letter #47

Gray nap of false dawn held in the glass of water I left beside the
lamp the night before. It's May. The moment in bed before we rise,
when dream has not yet given way to what we can bite into. Or a thin
taper – skittish flame, and, in any breath, only the smoke-tail of some
burrowing animal.

The trick of May is to believe with empty hands. And then always,
after we fail at faith, small-fires of crocus or bluebell snag the eye. But
Cory it's been raining for weeks and

elms are old men sitting on the porch of the local hotel. Cartilage-
worn, they hum country songs of bone on bone. This is all

there is. You told me once that sky in the May of your childhood,
Grenfell, south of Regina, is the colour of your old blue t-shirt. Maybe
someone has said it better, you thought. Maybe not.

Somewhere I read that Renoir believed what survives the artist is the
feeling he gives through objects. This morning, stretched across its
heart, sky wears a t-shirt rubbed butterfly-thin by so many slow
Saturday mornings, coffee and a newspaper, sleep-thick limbs.

Cory it's been raining for weeks, but as I write this two boys throw
a tennis ball at a garage door. Small-fire pulse of sun at the corner of
eye. This is all there is. I have travelled for a season and at the end of
my hunger, who could imagine

such abundance! A last swallow of cold coffee, the slap of boy-shouts
and a ball. Sky, old-t-shirt blue, woven of so-many petals of rain.

That song that goes

For no reason I can name
I look away from the book and see
the moon deepen into golds and reds.
Eastern sky a sodden blue. Spring
dusk is something to breathe deeply –
wet dirt, stubble, last year's leaves.
And like a dream that comes back
only when unasked for, I recall
his hands from when I was a child –
rough wood, tobacco, metal of earth.
A friend tells me of early grey mornings
at his kitchen table. There was tea,
the beginnings of a wood-fire, his wife,
bread. And the winter riverbed, the long,
slow ache I carry inside, briefly fills
with the singing of Spring melt.
Memory is that song the heart hums
along with. The one without
thinking, beneath breath.

Come

: I will follow you, I said, to a place where night is a season,
where the horizon is as fine as, beneath a lover's hand,
lacing on a chemise. I will follow you to a city sewn
by river, where we'll stand on a canal, your hands
warming in my coat, horizon open, our faces
in a constellation of snow and stars.
I will follow you to where there is no parting,
to a city sewn by river, horizon spilling
snow, spilling stars, your hands warming
in my coat, near a river, for a season,
for an hour.

Come,
you said,

Come.

Ash, Smoke

wait. My grandfather's crop is in so my dad can work road crew. Sixteen hour days driving grader. Saving eight bucks an hour to buy his own place. NW 18 36 22 W2nd. A name that will mark distance. But now, I imagine him humming small songs that mean home:

work boots by a door; kitchen window frost; honey and tea; his hands unclenching against her breasts; stars. I've never really listened to his stories so

I don't know where he is, but July sun, a whetstone, thins his body. Later scars of heat, sweat, clay, splintered trees are totem to what breaks him. His eyes, the colour of a palmed drink from slough.

After, he'll drink whisky, woman-hand warm, to *sshh* away the many-million insect shriek of machine. To ease his bones into the camp's plywood bunk bed: hot cup, night window, his hands, her breasts, stars. He is mad with grief, but

no one believes him. I've never listened to his stories, but there is no time for shame. Someone has thrown me in front of his blade. Throat, bare mirror in sun. *Quick!* I'll be ground into soil. Ash, smoke of an old war. My heart, clipped-

tongue, caws for air. *Quick!*

Somewhere a man digs dirt in heat. Sweat, clay, splinters, leaves in his hair. Plough on rock. He knows there will be ash, smoke. Woman-hands. Whisky. Shriek of machine. And after that his name will mark distance. It'll break him,

but no one believes. He is mad with grief. Why does he stop ploughing? Jump off the grader? Wipe dirt from my eyes? By my name he gives up so much. *sshh*. There is no time for shame. *Now*

Notes

The epigraph at the beginning of the book is from an early draft of Anne Simpson's poem "Dunn's Beach". The final version of the poem can be found in Simpson's book, *Quick* (McClelland and Stewart, 2007).

"Lastochka" makes reference to the 900 day siege of St. Petersburg by Nazi Germany. On September 8, 1941, the Germans fully encircled St. Petersburg and the siege began. It lasted until January 27, 1944. During the winter of 1941-42, there was no heat, little food, and almost no electricity.

Palace Square – Originally the palace of Tsar Peter the Great that overlooks the Neva. Now a museum called the Hermitage. The square is a centre for city gatherings.

Shostakovich – Russian composer, Dmitri Shostakovich (1906-1975).

Ciurlionis – Lithuanian artist and composer, Mikalojus Konstantinas Ciurlionis (1875-1911).

Ghe – Russian painter, Nicholas Ghe (1831-1894).

"Bird-bones" is for Andrew Benning.

"Amber" — *Kazanski Sabore* is the Kazanski Cathedral, St. Petersburg, Russia. *Letney-Sad* are the Summer Gardens, a park of Peter the Great's that faces the Neva.

"The Breath of Looking" is for Don McKay and Tim Lilburn in thanks for the Nature Writing Colloquium, St. Peter's College and Abbey, Muenster SK, 2001.

"unsent letter #28" is for Sarah Tsiang.

"Legato" is for Stan Dragland.

"unsent letter #47" is for Cory Wolfe.

Acknowledgments

While completing this manuscript, my work appeared in *Grain, Prism international, Event, Arc, The Malahat Review*, CV2, *Other Voices, Prairie Fire, A Room of One's Own, The Antigonish Review, Echolocation, Forget, The Fieldstone Review, The Fiddlehead, The New Quarterly*; and in the anthologies *Listening with the Ear of the Heart* (St. Peter's Press 2003), *Breathing Fire 2: Canada's New Poets* (Nightwood Editions 2004), *Third Floor Lounge* (littlefishcart Press 2004), and *Fast Forward: New Saskatchewan Poets* (Hagios Press 2007). A suite of poems was broadcast on CBC Saskatchewan's *Gallery*. Several poems appeared in a chapbook, *The Breath of Looking* (JackPine Press), designed by Rosalie and Heather Benning. My great appreciation to everyone involved.

I wish to thank The Canada Council for the Arts and the Saskatchewan Arts Board for providing financial assistance. Thanks also to the Banff Writing Studio, the Sagehill Writing Experience, the University of New Brunswick, the University of Alberta and to the good people therein.

I am indebted to those who attended to the thinking along the way – especially Dan Ahern, Tim Lilburn, Anne Simpson and Demetres Tryphonopoulos. Stan Dragland and Barry Dempster's early encouragement of this manuscript made a difference.

Warm thanks to Maureen and Kitty who've been a joy to work with, and to Grant McConnell for generously providing the cover image.

Special gratitude to Don McKay for his exceptional editorial care, and for those hikes he took me on.

I am also grateful to Sarah Tsiang and Tim McIntyre for sharing this and everything else with me, to Mina Tobin for walking with me those first few months, and to Rosalie Benning for her boundless support.

As always, to my family, for the stories we share.